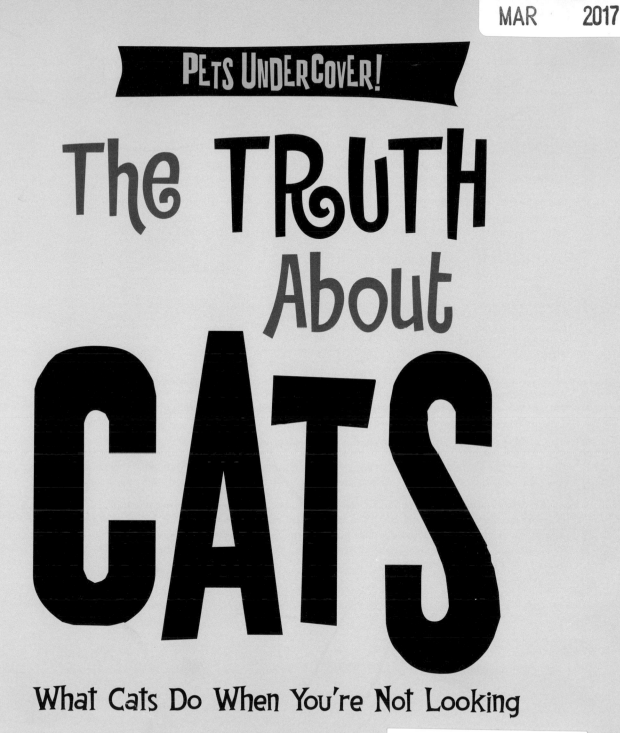

PETS UNDERCOVER!

The TRUTH About CATS

What Cats Do When You're Not Looking

MARY COLSON

capstone

© 2017 Heinemann-Raintree
an imprint of Capstone Global Library, LLC
Chicago, Illinois

To contact Capstone Global Library please call 800-747-4992, or visit our web site
www.mycapstone.com

Edited by Helen Cox Cannons
Designed by Philippa Jenkins
Picture research by Morgan Walters
Production by Laura Manthe
Originated by Capstone Global Library Ltd
Printed and bound in Canada
10038S17

Library of Congress Cataloging-in-Publication Data
Cataloging-in-publication information is on file with the Library of Congress.
Written by Mary Colson.
ISBN 978-1-4109-8605-4 (library binding)
ISBN 978-1-4109-8617-7 (eBook PDF)

Acknowledgments
We would like to thank the following for permission to reproduce photographs: All photographs
by Capstone Studio: Karon Duke; Shutterstock: (cat face) 19.

We would like to thank Ryan Neile for his help in the preparation of this book.

Every effort has been made to contact copyright holders of any material reproduced in this book.
Any omissions will be rectified in subsequent printings if notice is given to the publisher.

In memory of Otis

Some words are shown in bold, **like this**. You can find
out what they mean by looking in the glossary.

TABLE oF ConTEnts

Hello!

Meow! My name is Otis. It's so nice to meet you. I'm going to tell you all about myself and my many talents.

You will find I'm pretty incredible. I mean, look at me. Have you ever seen anything quite so purr-fect? I know I look silky smooth, but I'm actually really wild.

Breakfast Time

I live with my owners, Anna and Ben, and their parents. As they get my breakfast, I rub against their legs. I put my **scent** on them to say that they are my friends. I have **scent glands** all over my body and lots in my chin and cheeks.

After everyone has left for school and work, I have a very busy day ahead of me.

Keeping Clean

It takes a lot of cleaning to look this good! My tongue is rough, like sandpaper. I use it to clean off any dirt.

My own **scent** helps me to **communicate** with other cats. It tells them about who I am and where I've been.

Scratch Attack!

That's better! I do love a good scratch. A sofa, a chair—anything will do!

I like to scratch against furniture to keep my claws short and sharp. I never know when I might need them! I even have my own **scratch post**.

Jumping High

Look at me jump! I am an amazing athlete. I can jump up to six times my own height in a single leap. Can you? Of course not! You're only a human.

We cats have super-strong **hind legs**. Our tails help us balance too. I like to be high up to see what's going on.

Ready to Attack

Behind all this fluff, I'm wild at heart. If I notice something such as a fly moving, I **stalk** it. Why do I do this? I'm hunting. I practice stalking all the time with my toys. I lie very still. I am very **patient**. I watch and wait until I am ready to attack.

Leaping into Action

I have super-quick **reflexes** and very strong muscles. These help me to pounce on my **prey**. Got it!

My whiskers help me to hunt too. They sense **vibrations** in the ground when prey is near. They also help me judge space and distance. This is how I know whether I can squeeze through a gap.

Chasing Away Danger

Hiss! Hiss! Who's that outside the window? Get out of my **territory**!

The fur on my back sticks up when I'm defending myself. My tail shows how I'm feeling too. I swish my tail when I'm scared or angry. I'm a speedy runner if I'm chasing something.

Hiss! Go away!

What Does My Purr Mean?

I purr when I'm being pet by Anna or Ben. I also purr when I'm in pain or upset. If Anna or Ben pet me when I'm sore, I scratch them. I don't mean to hurt them—it's a **reflex**.

Other kinds of cats, such as lions and tigers, can't purr. That's why pet cats like me are just purr-fect!

Time for a Nap

We cats need our beauty sleep!
Our busy lives are just *so* tiring.
I can sleep anywhere. You might
find me snoozing on your bed
(or in other places I'm not
supposed to be).

I sleep for at least 12 hours a day.
I'm not always in a deep sleep
though. I'm always ready to leap
up if danger is near!

Watching and Waiting

Isn't it funny how I'm always at the door when you come home? I know you're coming. My hearing is one of my superpowers! The shape of my ears means I can hear things long before humans can. I can also hear much higher noises than you can.

Hi, Anna and Ben! Meow!

When You Go to Sleep...

At nighttime, I like to snoop around. I practice hunting at dawn and **dusk**. One of the many amazing things about me is my eyes. My **pupils** are much bigger than yours. This means I can still see in places where there isn't much light.

In the morning, Anna and Ben find me snoozing in my bed. They don't know what I have been up to all night. A new day and a new adventure awaits!

How Wild is *Your* Cat?

1. What does your cat do when it senses danger?

   a) It licks its paws and starts cleaning itself.

   b) It crouches down to hide away.

   c) Its whiskers twitch and its fur stands up. It's ready to leap away!

2. What does your cat do when it sees another cat nearby?

   a) It hides away in its basket.

   b) It shows it isn't bothered and ignores it.

   c) It watches and checks the new cat out. Sometimes it hisses.

3. How does your cat play with a toy mouse?

a) It pushes it under the couch.

b) It sits and waits for it to do something.

c) It stalks it before pouncing on it and biting it.

4. What does your cat do to mark its territory?

a) It sleeps in as many places as possible.

b) It walks around a lot.

c) It rubs its cheeks and chin on you and the furniture. Now you all smell the same. You are in the gang!

To find out how wild your cat is, check the results on page 32.

Glossary

communicate (kuh-MYOO-nuh-kate)—share information or feelings

dusk (DUHSK)—the time of day after sunset when it is almost dark

hind leg (HINDE LEGG)—the back legs of an animal

patient (PAY-shunt)—able to stay calm and relaxed

prey (PRAY)—animal hunted and eaten by another animal

pupil (PYOO-puhl)—black spot in the middle of your eye

reflex (REE-fleks)—an action that happens without a person's control or effort

scent (SENT)—the smell of something

scent gland (SENT GLAND)—a special organ in the body that create smells

scratch post (SKRACH POHST)—an upright piece of wood covered with carpet for pets to scratch against

stalk (STAWK)—to hunt an animal in a quiet, secret way

territory (TER-uh-tor-ee)—an area of land that an animal claims as its own to live in

vibration (vye-BRAY-shuhn)—a fast movement back and forth

Find Out More

Books

Gardeski, Christina Mia. *Cat Care*. Cats, Cats, Cats. North Mankato, Minn.: Capstone, 2017.

Guillain, Charlotte. *Cats*. Animal Family Albums. Chicago: Raintree, 2013.

Hamilton, Sue L. *Cats*. Xtreme Pets. Minneapolis, Minn.: ABDO Publishing, 2014.

Internet Sites

FactHound offers a safe, fun way to find Internet sites related to this book. All of the sites on FactHound have been researched by our staff.

Here's all you do:

Visit *www.facthound.com*

Type in this code: 9781410986054

 Check out projects, games and lots more at
www.capstonekids.com

Index

Quiz Answers:

Mostly As: Are you sure that you have a cat and not a mouse? You've got the softest, tamest cat in the world!

Mostly Bs: Your cat is pretty wild. It likes to be active but isn't keen on facing up to danger.

Mostly Cs: Your cat is as wild as they come! It's ready to take on anything! In fact, it's just a whisker away from being a lion!